BREAKWATER BOOKS LTD.

BREAKWATER BOOKS LTD.
100 Water Street • P.O. Box 2188 • St. John's • NL • A1C 6E6
www.breakwaterbooks.com

Library and Archives Canada Cataloguing in Publication

Pratt, Christopher, 1935-
    A painter's poems / Christopher Pratt.
ISBN 1-55081-152-5
    I. Title.

PS8581.R373P34 2005   C811'.54   C2005-904812-3
© 2005 Christopher Pratt

All images by the Author
Author's photograph: Ned Pratt
Design & Layout: Rhonda Molloy
Editor: Tom Henihan

ALL RIGHTS RESERVED. No part of this publication may be reproduced stored in a retrieval system or transmitted, in any form or by any means, without the prior written consent of the publisher or a licence from The Canadian Copyright Licensing Agency (Access Copyright). For an Access Copyright licence, visit www.accesscopyright.ca or call toll free to 1-800-893-5777.

We acknowledge the financial support of
The Canada Council for the Arts for our publishing activities.

We acknowledge the financial support of
the Government of Canada through the
Book Publishing Industry Development
Program (BPIDP) for our publishing activities.

Printed in Canada.

I am indebted to Breakwater Books, especially to Clyde Rose and Wade Foote, who have stuck with me with patience and forbearance through the many seasons of 'Will I - won't I's' that have preceded the publication of these poems.

I thank the friends who have encouraged me to get on with it, and equally those who, with as much good will, have counseled me otherwise.
Thanks to Melissa Nance for her input into the selection of these poems and most especially to my Editor, the poet Tom Henihan, without whose insight, understanding, guidance and solidarity this book would not have seen the light of day.

It is dedicated to the people, imaginary or real, who – and without their leave – inhabit it. They appear as actors, hopefully well cast.

Christopher Pratt
July 7, 2005
Salmonier

October is the Ocean's Spring

October is the ocean's spring,
it feeds the sea,
cuts the carcass from tidewater flats
and fires my winter whims.

March brought life back to the land
across bakeapple bogs
by hunchbacked junipers,
and acid spruce.

April sent long sinews
through rich fields furrowed under kelp.
Then, with orange-autumn gales
stinging, flinging salt,

I dream of black ducks
blown through wild blue skies.
At peace I watch the ravens gorge
and sing of summer running down the rocks.

© C. Pratt 1953

How Soon When the Day is White

How soon when the day is white
and a raw wind whines in the raven's sticks,
my lonely heart will swell with the empty air
of pains and pleasures past
and I would live again every half forgotten year.

Quick as grey birds spread their yawning wings
and ride the seaweed-smelling fog
to where the caplin casts her seed across the sand,
the wind-eyed boys have fled the Friday hills.
And some will come to know the cold of men
whose footsteps ring across the frozen decks
of steamers in the Straits
above the roar of tide tormented ice
they only hear the foghorns belching from the capes.
Into the hollow night they strain poor eyes,
their spirit borne, their vision dimmed by hope.

Will I have wandered all my life along these barren cliffs
feeling the green air rip the brittle bark
from trees bleached white as lambs' bones by the wind,
hearing the sea asleep along the land,
the chatter of a thousand birds,
loving every brazen cry. And I will sing of women
where they bend to Autumn bogs
wringing summer from the tired sods.

I only feel the dawn's light lap alive upon the black bay's rim.
Snipe in the morning marsh, wing your wild song
down the swollen April brooks for me.
All that I ever was I am, and all that I can ever hope to be.

© C. Pratt 1954

The Apples

Too timid in the afternoons
to run across the open fields
we waited by the willow rows and watched
green apples shining in the sun

but when the early darkness came
as brave as ghosts
we raced across the meadows to the trees
and in the privacy of night

our fingers felt along
the promise of the apple limbs
until the ripening apples lay
cupped in the hollows of our hands.

© C. Pratt ca. 1954

You Came to Me

You came to me so gently
I thought that life itself was greeting me.
Your fingertips passed over me
as breezes break the mirror of the pond
and cause the light to shiver across grass.

© C. Pratt 1963

It Happened Slowly

It happened slowly
yet suddenly I realized
the snow had melted and become
the blossoms on an apple tree.

It happened very slowly
yet suddenly I know
that there are blood-red apples
underneath the snow.

© C. Pratt 1963

Orion: Residue of Fire

What but the residue of fire
the forge of molten iron
remaining at the heart
when all things otherwise
have lost all trace of that transition
into being – what else
could keep us warm against the universe.

Bitter cloudless winter nights
the ice-lights of Orion mocking us
the interstellar threat, absolute zero
pouring down our backs
as draughts and fear of enemies
and ghosts, all things unknown
bristle, chill.

I can see why horned owls kill
and bring what Hemingway had called
"the gift of death" by
as if to celebrate
light of earth's moon, life's nemesis –

And I
understand the physics of reflected light
sterile, inorganic, white,
and spring-tides flooding in response to gravity.
But not so easily
why dogs and foxes bark
and lovers in each others' arms obey.

© C. Pratt 1965

First Communion

Finally
the night preceding Christmas Eve
pent up anticipation
pumping high adrenalin
the pit of my courage well fuelled
burning hot, finally
I ventured calling you and you said yes.
Flooded, flushed, I celebrated with
a strange, at-hand communion:
a Coca-Cola,
and some mustard on a hot dog roll.

© C. Pratt 1966

Looking Back

Looking back
I can't remember if it was
an evening late in spring or early in the fall
except that it was warm and it had rained

and when the light was gone
the darkness made a soft and silent room
so close around us that we were its walls.

© C. Pratt 1969

Now That the Light is Out

Now that the light is out
that made my windows
mirrors of my rooms
and drew
strange insects from the darkness
to my house,
I can at last see out
into the black
and crowded night.

© C. Pratt 1969

A Raven

A raven in a crooked pine
a sophomoric sort of line
but when you're heading down the hill
(the word I need right here is 'breath')
a raven in a pine is still
a quite convincing sign of death.

© C. Pratt 1970

Rosie's Song About the Rain

Have you seen the greens
in Newfoundland
she said:
have you noticed
how they seem illuminated
how they are stated
framed between the ash grey sky
the silver rivers, leaden lakes, the sea.

Have you seen the greens in winter
matted like watercolours by
the flake white snow
and skies of indigo
seen in summer
through the salt-white pickets
of a lilac fence
the grasses, monkshood
and the thistles there
beside the salt-lick headstones,
ferns, mosses, green.

Those lilacs are memorials
as monkshood and wild roses mark
abandoned properties
and lupins and wild parsnips often fill
cellars that have fallen in
there where lilacs are so lavender
washed lavender
and white-washed fences after rain –
don't you see they are memorials?

That was and so was everything:
therefor we wandered inland
through blueberry ground
burned, buzzing in the summer heat
and came upon dry peat bogs
shrivelled into dust
and peat ponds cracked,
crazed like antique porcelain
dessicated basins, brown.

Even from the forest floor
heat sprung
smelling like oakum, frankum, tar;
there, waiting rain
there, dormant talc-white lichens
dust-white dry
green, waiting for rain.

And you and me lying there
heat rising,
clean lavender
(did I say lavender before?)
the unexpected warmth,
earth like tinder
sunburned, bare.

Then with whimbrels assembling south,
and ravens riding uplift
on fall hurricanes, it rained:
the land the sea so green again.

"Have you tried Jasmine tea
and see I bought a green douvet
the other day looks good
don't you think what say
fern green no softer moss –
moss green."

Do you remember then
the warmth, the wisdom of it all:
heat rising there, the forest floor
(did I say lavender before?)
and have you seen – I mean,
the green –
the greens in Newfoundland she said.

© C. Pratt 1972

Had You Been With Me

Had you been with me
this morning when the breeze was fresh
you would have seen
my sails were sheeted drawing full
my little boat careened across the bay

and all around
was froth and foam and freedom
all around was salt and celebration
sharp, intoxicating wind
and seaways shivering with light.

In this warmth
this windless August afternoon
we float like sleeping birds
adrift between infinities
where clouds conspire with jellyfish
drifting through our shadow on the sky.

The only movement is a souvenir
of distant storms somewhere at sea
wilder even than the wind
you would have seen
had you been with me.

© C. Pratt 1972

Every Spring

Every spring
it's the same thing
burning boughs
off beds of frozen daffodils
unsheltering the climbing rose.

Every spring
it's the same thing
dense fat smoke
the sudden tongue of flame
hot grey cone of ash
the ring of unburnt wood
around the heart.

It's that ring:
the greatest satisfaction
is to rake it in, to see
the last loose ends consumed.
It's the same thing
every spring.

© C. Pratt 1972

Waiting, Then, is Two Things

Before you come
I will have waited years,
seen cars flood the road with light
only to disappear into the night.

When you come
by then I will have heard
cars stop a thousand times
heard doors open, footsteps on the ground,
only to realize the forest made the sound.

Waiting, then, is two things:
One, for dawn, or death – for certainty
Two, the waiting that I do for you.

© C. Pratt 1973

I Know Winter is Coming

I know winter is coming.
I know how early we will be awake
that morning of the strange new light,
how it will smell so clean,
the first snow covering the grass,
the leaves, the overtired earth.
And I anticipate a silence then,
the summer birds departed
and all the insects stilled.
I know it is coming.
In all likelihood you will go away.

© C. Pratt 1975

Fall Fish

Fall-fat female
red with
ripe with roe,
belly bursting
furrowing deep redds
pebbles, silt
roiling peat-stained waters,
bloodshot
swollen vent distended,
issuing.

Male, hook-jawed jack
sides all sucked in
gaping, slack
oozing afterwards
residual,
anaemic milt
mixing
blood red, blood white,
torn fin,
tail,
furrow, fill.

They fell downstream
slinking, spent
rolling belly-up
glaze-eyed, fish-eyed, tail-first
into the sea again.

© C. Pratt 1976

I Find it Strange

I find it strange so suddenly
to be surrounded by things
I have used for years,
seeing their edges round
noticing that in my hand
these tools erode,
that I not only die
but also must participate in time.

© C. Pratt 1976

The Rat

After all that
about the courage of a cornered rat
you cowered in your hole shivering.

You hid
your small rat-head behind a junction box
shielding your red rat-eyes
against the fingers of my light.

You cringed,
you didn't turn to face the stick
that broke your hunched rat-back.

Coward rat,
you lost your small rat-life cornered,
your rat-heart didn't turn to fight
but whimpered at the challenge of my light.

© C. Pratt 1979

I Watched You Walking on the Tantramar

I watched you walking on
the Tantramar,
leaving me alone
with nothing but
the vast low silence of the wind
and marsh birds calling.

I watched you walking
infinitely small,
smaller than
the marsh birds,
smaller even than
the droning insects,
dung-flies, ants.

And I could see
how God
could focus everything
all being, life
the universe,
all secrets in
one sub-atomic particle,
which you became,
walking smaller on the marsh.

© C. Pratt 1982

Such Was the Way of It

The birds rang like so many bells
through those evenings
echoing through thin stands of birch
and sparse evergreens,
the cliffs and granite outcroppings
doubling their chime.

Such was the way of it,
its substance dependent on
the echoing, the mirroring, the doubling.
It seemed insufficient in itself,
insubstantial, two-dimensional,
needing repetition to exist.

Tell me, do you understand one word of that?
I am rambling. I repeat myself.

© C. Pratt 1984

My Father Used to Listen to the Wilderness

My father used to listen
to the wilderness
night after night,
he never tired of it.

It seemed to satisfy
his need for loneliness:
the melodrama of a loon
occasionally, snipe
winnowing in May and June.

But always it was voices
that he listened for
trying to translate the language
of the wind and forest
heard like conversation
in a nearby room.

I have not admitted this before,
but when he died,
before they took his casket
to the church,
I met with him alone
and said what I would call a prayer
and rapped three times
on the coffin lid:
Father, Son and Holy Ghost.

Since then
I have listened to the land
night after night, I never tire of it
and listened in my room
willing to accept the smallest sign:
three snipe winnowing at once,
three trucks in tandem on the road,
three clouds across the moon
but never hearing anything.

Sometimes I talk to him
trying to explain what's going on
knowing that I'm talking to myself
and listening for voices
in the wilderness.

© C. Pratt 1984

Ranger

Ocean, raging
flaming
smoking like a fire
whipped across
monstrous
dessicated planes
of ancient grass
the mythic sea of grain
flaming phosphorescent
frigid
green.

They fell –
like wingshot waterfowl
they fell into a sea
where even death
held one last treachery –
behold
the fires
the furnaces
the very flames of hell
were cold.

© C. Pratt 1984

On Coley's Point: For Irene and Elizabeth

You will have noticed
if you notice anything
I visit only when
the ground is warm
only when the berries form
wax white, flushed rose
promising blue, alluding to
the promise of rebirth
the rhetoric of resurrection
from bad earth.

© C. Pratt 1984

Sorry, Nothing Ventured, Nothing Gained

Sorry, nothing ventured nothing gained.
Immaculate blue sky, bright diamond fired sun
and yet it rained.

All that year the crows flew singly,
never in two or three.
One for sorrow, one for me.

She said, "just wave at them as they go by."
I waved ... they must have been too high
but so would I if I could fly.

I said, "perhaps I'll be like Icarus and try,
and if like him I soar too near the sun
and melt, and fall, and die..."

and she said "why"?

© C. Pratt 1984

You Came Into My Studio

You came into my studio and said:
those tones, especially the reds,
are stronger than the ones you've used before.

I said: my eyes aren't what they used to be
and there are things I want to see, there's nothing more.

You said: that music is much louder than is usual for you.
I said: I think that too much subtlety can be deceit –
besides, I want to feel the music through my feet.

You saw me rip the drawing I was working on in two;
You said: that's new, not a thing you used, or ought, to do.

I said: I'm tired of a lot of things, of colours I can't see,
sounds too delicate to hear, things out of focus, out of range
the vanishing remains of what I hoped would be,
but most of all reality.

You said, I thought sarcastically:
"Poor me"?

© C. Pratt 1984

I Have More Evidence of You

My heart broke its promises to you
before the words were dry upon my lips.

I have more evidence of you than I can bear
among my souvenirs
and you have evidence of me.

No point remembering –
everything is now, not what it used to be.
I only see the things you left behind.

© C. Pratt 1984

The Grouse: Words Come So Easily

I saw a little tragedy,
perhaps anthropomorphically,
but picture this:

Hen grouse, a clutch of golf-ball chicks,
bewildered by the black expanse
of flat unshielding road open to the sky.

Imagine then a tractor-trailer rig,
40,000 kilograms of furnace oil
doing 95 kilometers,
barrelling (words come so easily)
just barrelling along no way to stop
not even if it wanted to.

The hen, cowering on the road
counting on her camouflage
instantly is history, mashed flat,
the chicks rip in the vortex
for two hundred yards.
The scale of the thing, the overkill.

Words come so easily.

© C. Pratt 1986

Poem for an Aging Artist

I watched you come on stage
and couldn't overlook the evidence,
that slow arthritic gait.

But when you played it came to me
that you had rationed your mobility,
saved all urgency to invest it in your hands.

You reminded me of a reservoir
– Grand Coulee Dam! –
spilling music through your fingertips.

Therefore, life may yet prove to be a reservoir,
a cornucopia that yields its riches in reverse,
focused, concentrated at the end.

© C. Pratt 1986

I Had Already Written Poetry for You

I had already written poetry for you.
I had said, rhetorically,
you were a symphony of pink and gold,
a song of white and blue.

Forgive me my small jealousies.
I could not bear to think of you
in someone else's arms
for all you shielded me from that reality
I feared the silent evidence
the echo of a foreign substance on your lips,
a different rhythm on your breath.

Did I tell you that one night I dreamed
about a perfect meadow, shining, square,
polished by the sharp salt air
filled everywhere with flowers and waving grass –
it didn't seem that anyone had trodden there.

You brought me petals every morning,
fresh, until I held them angled to the light
where I could see that something
had passed over them at night.

© C. Pratt 1986

The Gannet: When it is a Memory

When it is a memory
where will that white bird,
in what sea,
will she dip her ink-black primaries

what weightless creature
will be spared
the terror
of that glazed, emphatic eye,
that flesh-blue beak.

© C. Pratt 1986

Wind in Dry Grass

Wind in dry grass
that rustling, breathing sound
the friction of one dehydrated shaft
against another, I suppose –

a million little slaps;
and in the distance
sounds of fall seas breaking
rattling down a cobble beach.

If needs be that reminds me
summers come and go
and love is long
but not forever necessarily.

© C. Pratt 1990

When I See My Friends

When I see my friends asleep,
I notice how their softened faces
loose all lift, all animation,
all of youth's leavening.

When I see my friends asleep
I must acknowledge death's proximity.

© C. Pratt 1990

Imitating New

My hands recently dulled,
thickened by unaccustomed work
have come to know you differently,
as if you were wrapped
in soft brushed cotton.

What is the meaning
of this slight annulment
of the sense of touch?
Is it the mystery
of something seen at dusk,
half-seen by half-light,
the river rattling,
voices imagined in the trees,
or conversations caught
above the babble of a crowd,
leaving much to the imagination
like the late Impressionists.

Promise, anticipation,
said so often to exceed fulfillment,
perhaps this blunted insight
is the best of it
or more simply put, has it to do
with the unexpected imitating new.

© C. Pratt 1992

A Song for Billy McNeil

Billy, you're only a snapshot to me
of a beautiful girl by the Miramichi
with a great whopping salmon just brought to the gaff
and your whole life ahead, when it still was a laugh.

What do you say to the nurse on the floor
who was trained by the Mission on bleak Labrador
when you hear her boast to her peers in the hall
that "Billy looks bad, but I've seen it all".

And you know what she means, and it's certainly true
that she has seen people in worse shape than you:
dismembered miners, and fishermen found
entangled in twine months after they drowned.

And girls dead in childbirth and boys white with fear
and disease-ravaged women with death stalking near
lying in squalor with nothing to give
where fear will not die and hope cannot live.

And you know she's seen icebergs shimmering white
transparent as emeralds and indigo nights
and the sun rising over the Labrador sea,
and King Eiders flying, and deer running free.

And you know she's smelled birches and bogs after rain,
and slept on the land that her God gave to Cain
with a crowberry-mattress and grey sky above
and there with the land and a landsman made love.

But she didn't see that bright day in July –
the swift swelling river, the sweep of your fly,
the swirl of the fish and your reel singing free
on that day, in that year, on the Miramichi.

© C. Pratt 1993

Good Friday

Pale infertile earth
frozen hard as flint
three feet down
and under that rude rubble,
grey stones only.

And I could get no sense
of resurrection from that burial,
no sense that what had gone to earth
could ever rise again.

This was not resurrection's fertile plane.
Ashes to ashes then, and dust to dust –
atoms into atoms let us say,
reason into rock.

© C. Pratt 1994

Lying on the Settle

Lying on the settle facing south
the January sun pokes at his eyes
through panes of wrinkled glass.

The settle smells
like something from a harness shop
and half a century of cooking
salt fish on a softwood fire.

The heat, the sunlight
wakes a blue-tailed fly.
He hears it buzzing, buzzing by
above the silence of the clock.

And then he hears
wind rattling the aspen leaves
a white-throat calling
and a distant ovenbird.

And so he owes his last summer day
to one fly buzzing,
turning January into May.

© C. Pratt 1994

Twice Fine Fish: At Salmonier

I hooked a twice fine fish
just above the running-out
'tide-water pool', we called it then.

It didn't really rise –
I was fishing with a large grey ghost,
two hooks, tandem-tied –
it assailed the fly and in that
lurched across the ledge into the sea,
bearing deep into the undertow
riding the massive current out.

I can still feel
the heavy throbbing of its travel
shouldering my line
into the sea's dark uterine depths
until it broke. Its soul it seems
was not inclined to humour mine.

© C. Pratt 1996

Fishing With Bob

Forty minutes walking
maybe thirty more to go
bush, bog, windfall
tiring; and every time
we stopped to catch our breath
we started teasing Bob
about his clothes. We said
he looked like he was going
to play golf.

He didn't wear a tackle vest
and had a salt-and-pepper hat
that mocked the shapeless quiffs
we wore pretentiously festooned
with flies. But it was his refusal
to wear high wading boots
that left him looking like a golfer
in plus-fours, his trousers tucked
into his knee high socks
with only canvas sneakers
on his feet.

I envied that. I knew that he
could feel the rhythms of the land
would know the roll and tumble
of the riverbed. I don't believe
the fact he's crippled with arthritis now
has got a lot to do
with wading glacial rivers
on the coast of Labrador
in stockings, not much more –
although I do remember
Doc Collingwood predicted it.

© C. Pratt 1996

Because You Gave Me Blue

July has me remembering
the summer life was new,
the land, the sea and everything
the time you gave me blue.

The dress you wore became the sky
your fragrance was its hue,
you changed the colours of my eye
because you gave me blue.

The devil's paintbrush was in flame,
the daisies loved me true,
I heard the grasses breathe my name
the day you gave me blue.

Oh, when you gave me blue the night
was rich with lilac-wine,
the sky was indigo and white
and all of it was mine.

© C. Pratt 1996

A Note Left for You

I think of you downstairs
in your small room
you monitor your privacy
listening for voices overhead,
typing silently – cat's paws
tapping on computer keys.

And I, narcissistically
imagine you reading through
this poetry, watching my words
come up on the screen
like Michelangelo discovering
David standing in the stone.

I watch you with what seems to be
prodigious aptitude, commend
ideas inherited from lamplight
to the frigid memory
of new technologies.
Nonetheless
my instinct is to say Amen.

© C. Pratt 1996

Remembering Henry at Horton's

Henry,
having little access to pornography
(his mother ran a tight ship and his dad
gave at the office, so to speak)
ogled through the ladies pages
in old Eaton's catalogues,
occasionally considered bathing suits,
but mostly underwear; and later on
began his nightly raids on laundry lines –
keeping his collection
hidden in the blue and orange boxes
from his Lionel trains.

We got talking about that
me and Pete and Jake
over large coffees and three sour-cream glazed,
loosening our black ties
at a Horton's afterwards
and the time Hen traded
twenty minutes riding his new Hercules
with Marg, for one five minute feel
and Marg, delivering, ripped-off his watch.

Jake recalled
Hen telling us about that later on –
not that Hen, ordinarily, was one to blab –
if anything he thrived, was 'turned on' by
a bit of secrecy
but there are situations when
a kid needs currency, a special entry
and eventually, Hen – wanting to buy in –
described how Marg closed shop,
precisely at five minutes flat,
timed with his own watch, that was that,
made tracks – wouldn't let him fish it
from the pocket of her slacks.

Of course
we didn't use expressions like
'ripped-off' and 'turned-on'.
We had a reservoir of less
and more descriptive wartime words
out of context, frequently misunderstood
so when Pete said
he always figured Henry must be gay
(he had that Liberace look –
a dash of Danny Kaye)
Jake had to say:
we would have called him queer, I guess
gay just meant happy then.
We all agreed that happy
wasn't quite the word for Hen.

I said, I often wondered,
why we gave Henry so much flack;
we were only kids, Jake said
and Christ! kids can be cruel
dish out more than they can take
to cover insecurities
repeat things they hear adults say
just for effect: one thing age teaches you
is to respect respect.

Pete
went and got two muffins and a maple dip
"fresh out of the oven" he declared
I rolled up my rim but didn't win –
Jake got three more coffees,
checked his watch, and said:
"They're probably just puttin' Henry in."

© C. Pratt 1996

Time Warp on the Tantramar

I went walking on the High Marsh Road
a hay-wagon laboured with a heavy load
the barns bright shingled and their ridge-poles fair –
but a truck roared by that wasn't there.

Then the barn roofs sagged being made of tin
the end-boards rotted and the doors fell in
and the hay lay sodden by a century's rain
when a barn-owl hooted and it changed again.

And I heard geese honking and the cattails crack
and a steam engine whistle on a distant track
and I saw you walking on the Tantramar –
then I came to my senses and got in my car.

© C. Pratt 1996

God How I Hated Those Drab Years

God, how I hated those drab years.
A decade of drizzle it seems to me now:
Summer of misery, frost warnings in July,
eternal fog yet forest fires raged.
And afterwards the winters pelted sleet
denying the absolution of a foot of snow.
And small men sequestered in small rooms
boasting they had blinded us, put out our eyes,
winking at each other and their visitors
signifying they were the one-eyed leaders of the blind.
God, how I hated all of it! And me…?
not that it would have made a difference,
I ran away, escaped, found sanctuary
in the borough of geometry,
the precincts of straight lines.

© C. Pratt 1997

Black Night

Black night. Rain following late March snow
has washed the trees and boulders bare
so there is definition, visibility.

Wind batters my car.
I kill the engine, turn the headlights off
open the window on my side – just a crack.
Hear. See.

Huge bearded seas looming everywhere –
the wilderness of ocean, the universe,
the unimaginable - explode.

Foghorn moaning in the distance
is strangely reminiscent
of cattle lowing on the Tantramar.

The Cape Spear light
flashes three times, then occults,
three times, occults, three times…

The foghorn, even from this misery asserts
we are the healthy and the whole, the quick.
Hear us. Return.

Frail ships,
hearing nothing at their offing
fail, break, disintegrate into the palliative sea.

© C. Pratt 1998

I Never Asked You Why

I never asked you why
your eyes were always focused
on distances I knew could exist
only inside of you –
horizons being finite
and intervals of stars
measured with a metronome.

Distance and time were one in you
and always multiplied.
What was gone was gone
out the door, over the moon
behind the Great Bear's back –
last night, last year,
before the birth of Christ,
it made no difference.
No scale, no hourglass
would be appropriate
to measure your infinity.

Now it is too late
because you cannot tell me
if that unexpected laughter in your eyes
should be clinically described
seen as a function of
post-stroke impairment
to the left side of your brain.

No – you have crossed a line
and seen things that confirm
your life-long understanding of futility.

© C. Pratt 1999

Last Christmas

Yes, I will cut down
and decorate a tree
for the two thousandth time –
but, failing a second coming
this could be the end of it.

I am in need of that
nor will I be disillusioned
should this coming prove
to be the first.

Tell me:
to whom will we pray
when our requirement
is *for* a god.

© C. Pratt Christmas 2000

At the End of the World – In Tenebris III

(Explaining some of it to Clyde)

At the end of the world
this is how it's gonna' be:
an apple in the grass
and a snake up in a tree
and the learned still proclaiming
from their tenured stools
that they have all the answers
the rest of us are fools
and the rich will be richer
and the poor will still be poor
and the meek shall tap politely
on the tyrant's door
and the slaves will be in slavery
while believing they are free
and the lame will not walk
and the blind will not see
that heaven is a maypole
where the dancers do not know
that hell is an old man,
pissing in the snow.

© C. Pratt 2001

Six Hundred Apples

I dumped six hundred apples in the brook,
hard, green, worm-eaten crabs
useless for cider, jelly, applesauce.
Five hundred made it to the estuary,
the last four hours later than the first
and when the tide turned,
seventeen came back, all except two
hard by the shoreline where they left.
I puzzled over this: what was the message there –
what wisdoms, mathematics or philosophy,
what tower of insight could the mind erect?
My father, who was in the hardware trade,
looked up from sorting out his salmon flies and
said:"So tell me now, what else would you expect"?

© C. Pratt 2002

Explaining it All to Al

Remember that old joke
about the guy who never smoked
or screwed around,
whose doctor buddy told him
he would never die –
how could he, he had never lived!
You could laugh at that…
for me it was a little closer to the bone,
although I never thought
I could abstain from death.

And I did go for sixty once or twice:
each time, I held the five, jack, king
and ace of hearts – not odds
a seasoned gambler would consider lean.
I should have known
the joker couldn't understand
the cunning of the queen.

© C. Pratt 2002

The Eider Ducks

When the eider ducks fly down the river I will die.
Speak not of superstition or mythologies,
I am an elder now, am wise.
I know how things conspire, repeat
and I can read the signs, have an instinct
for their origins and ironies, cause and effect:
nights when rabbits run and owls hunt successfully,
moons on which the herrings shoal.
And I can say with certainty this winter will be wild
having seen three such Decembers since I was a child,
the same foreboding in the winter solstice.
No, do not ask me how I know or why,
but when the eider ducks fly down the river I will die.

© C. Pratt 2002

List of Illustrations

Gene Pool (1996) ...	1
Me and Others (1996) ...	7
Self Portraits with Ghosts (1996) ...	13
My Mother and Me: *The Child is Parent to the Man* (2004) ...	58

www.ingramcontent.com/pod-product-compliance
Lightning Source LLC
Chambersburg PA
CBHW060504110426
42738CB00055B/2614